The Phenomenology *of* Death,
Death Is Not the End of Life

Rev. Dr. Kirk Morton
With Foreword by: Rev. Duane E. Dickens Sr.

Copyright © 2024 by Dr. Kirk Morton

ISBN: 978-1-77883-414-1 (Paperback)

All rights reserved. No part of this publication may be reproduced, distributed, or transmitted in any form or by any means, including photocopying, recording, or other electronic or mechanical methods, without the prior written permission of the publisher, except in the case brief quotations embodied in critical reviews and other noncommercial uses permitted by copyright law.

The views expressed in this book are solely those of the author and do not necessarily reflect the views of the publisher, and the publisher hereby disclaims any responsibility for them.

BookSide Press
877-741-8091
www.booksidepress.com
orders@booksidepress.com

OTHER WORKS BY DR. KIRK MORTON

BIBLICAL NUGGETS: Daily Devotions for Everyday Life

The Discipline of Prayer for Spiritual Maturity, Church Growth, and General Blessings of the Cathedral Church (Dissertation Drew University, 2004)

CONTENTS

Foreword 6

Acknowledgments 8

Chapter 1:   The Phenomenon Of Death 10
                        What Is Sleep? 16
                        The Purpose Of Sleep 17

Chapter 2:   What Is Death? 19
                        The Mystery Of Death 21
                        The Authoritative Source Of Truth 22

Chapter 3:   Faith And Hope 25

Chapter 4:   Have Faith In God 29
                        We Die To Live 32
                        The Power Of The Holy Spirit 35
                        The Manifestation Of Faith 37

References 45

FOREWORD

Rev. Duane E. Dickens Sr.

Dr. Kirk Morton is one of the most remarkable men I know. He is a master wordsmith and has always had the ability to take concepts whether abstract or concrete and interpret those ideas bringing insight and enlightenment to inquiring minds. He established his faith in the Lord Jesus Christ many years ago, thereby sealing his name in the Lamb's Book of Life. God has truly blessed Dr. Morton with a great community of family and friends who have witnessed the fulfillment of his aspirations and dreams as an athlete, a scholar, an educator, a minister, and a wonderful person.

Since our days together as seminary students at Drew Theological Seminary in Madison, New Jersey, Dr. Morton has mesmerized me with his academic agility. There were many days when I would, upon arrival on campus from my home on Long Island, New York, meet with Dr. Morton then we'd go to class to have our minds sharpened and our faith stretched where we would wrestle with great ideas and thoughts. He and I would engage in lengthy conversations about issues ranging from social justice to liberation theology and to analyzing life events as they unfolded before us. I am still amazed at his wit, his critical thinking, and his compassion about addressing issues that affect the human life and conditions.

In this book, Dr. Morton addressed an issue that few have "boldly gone before" to address and to discuss in his own way the phenomenology of death—death is not the end of life. Dr. Morton courageously addressed a phenomenon that all life is affected by death. What lies before us in the pages ahead was an incredible fearless faith based on embracing what ultimately becomes the culmination and conclusion of understanding that death is not the end of life. It really is the beginning of our eternal life.

In a real sense, much of what the Scripture speaks to regarding death reminded me of what the great Greek philosopher Plato called "forms"—that is, this life is not ultimately reality but what is experienced the moment one sleeps or rests in the bosom of God's presence. The Apostle Paul gave us an even greater expression: "Behold, I tell you a mystery: We shall not all sleep, but we shall all be changed—in a moment, in the twinkling of an eye, at the last trumpet. For the trumpet will sound, and the dead will be raised incorruptible, and we shall be changed" (1 Cor. 15:51–52).

I highly commend Dr. Kirk Morton for embracing a subject and a reality that many were so fearful and witfully try to avoid. The fact is we are all going to die someday. Other will probably remember a kind gesture, our commitment to address serious problems in our broken world, perhaps they will remember something we said or did to help lighten their load by bringing a smile or a cheer to one's face and/or life. But in the end, the greatest reward will be to hear the Lord say, "Well done!"

To my friend of over thirty-five years, this book simply gives us another glimpse into the awesome man you are. We have experienced life's fine moments. and we have been genuine brothers during good days and bad days gone by. I'll always remember the people who meant the most to you, your dad, your mom, your siblings, and the people we met during and since our seminary day sat Drew. I was so proud of you when I watched you receive your Masters of Divinity degree which you definitely earned and your doctorate both with honors. Kirk, I love you, man. You are a scholar, an educator, a man of God, and most of all, my friend.

Your brother in Christ,
Duane
Special Assistant to the Sr. Pastor
First Baptist Church of Glenarden, Landover, Maryland

ACKNOWLEDGMENTS

I dedicate this book to my sister, Allison, a.k.a. "Allie Ballie," who passed in December 2010 from her battle with breast cancer. Oh how I miss you so, and I'm dedicating this book to you in your honor for how you loved and supported me, as well as all our other siblings with nothing but pure and eternal love you had for each of us individually and for all of us collectively as your siblings, "the six."

In addition, I dedicate this book to my other siblings: Davyd (Lynda), Lynn, Barbara Jean, and Helen, because of you, I am the man I am today, and I thank you all for your unfaltering love and support to me throughout the entirety of my life as well. Without my siblings having been in my life, I just don't know what my life would have been like today or the kind of person I would have become, but because of you, today I'm grateful to you all for having your love and support in my life today and always. I thank you all individually and all of you collectively, and I pray God's best for each of you as we continue to grow in the *faith* and love which our mother has left for us to grow in since 1979, when she left us to carry on without her and our dad (who left us in 1990 when he expired after mom).

Also I would like, this time, to thank my very good brother, Pastor Duane E. Dickens Sr., who wrote the foreword for this book, and I pray may God add a double blessing on your life for your response to this work as God did for Elisha when he took Elijah away from him to go and be with him in glory and as he rested from his labors here on earth (nor am I your Elijah or am I now planning on going anywhere in regard to leaving you on today). But I'm just saying.

Pastor Dickens and I met when we were both students at Drew University Theological Seminary. Pastor Dickens is now a staff pastor at the First Baptist Church of Glenarden, Maryland, where he serves as the special assistant to the senior pastor who is none other than the very right, Rev. John K. Jenkins Sr. I just wanted to thank God for our friendship, and as the Bible said it, and it is correct when it said, "There is a friend who will stick closer to you than a brother." I'm so proud to call you my friend and also as my brother…for life!

CHAPTER ONE

The Phenomenon of Death

This is the phenomenon of death—the observable facts which can be explained in the situations that life exists after death in the flesh have occurred. Phenomenology is the philosophical study of consciousness as experienced from a person's point of view. The central focus of this experience is the intentionality of the person, as it is being directed toward those experiences and/or facts about that object or subject being discussed in this case of death and life after death. Then the phenomena are the facts of those situations which can be observed that exist or is happening, especially when one explains the causes of those facts in those situations which are in question about death. Therefore, an understanding of life in the Spirit without faith, death in the natural, is the phenomenon, and the conscious study of death in the Spirit and in faith is the phenomenology of death.

Death is extremely difficult to handle, and it's very hard to comprehend for those who don't operate in faith and who do not walk in the Spirit. They usually misinterpret the consequences of sins in their lives and the lusts of the flesh thus, making the phenomenon of death even more difficult to comprehend especially the concept of life after death when the Spirit separates from the body, which is the thesis for this book and the primary cause for this body of work. Without exercising or having *faith*, life after death cannot be understood according to the Bible. It is still, even more, difficult to comprehend the entire study of life after death when it is solely based on a life that is contingent upon the basis of what one only sees in the physical world.

Even though the *will to live* is still greater than the *will to die*, regardless of whether you have chosen to live by the Spirit or not or to believe or not believe, this notion to live is still greater than the reality of dying. Because God created us in his image, which was and always has been his plan for us to live eternally with him, this notion of the *will* is furthery compounded by the fact that when one chooses to live by the flesh over and against the *will* of the spirit, this is what makes death even more complex because one does not possess the necessities of living after death without faith. And in order to comprehend life after death, *faith* is required.

When we choose to live our lives in and by the flesh alone, we lose the battle of life in the Spirit because there is no death in the Spirit, and this cannot be understood without faith. And according to Smith Wigglesworth, "Faith is the eternal nature of who God is. Faith is the living power revealed in (you) the moment you believe" (Wigglesworth pp. 717, 715), and life in the Spirit continues *even* after one dies in the natural (in the flesh). And this is the phenom- enology of death, because some people only believe in life in the flesh, as if that is actually seen in the natural is and/or as being what is ultimately as real. Life in the Spirit for them is then discounted because for them, only what they see is believable or is being interpreted as what is only real and since they don't believe in the things which are not seen and they don't exercise faith or won't believe nor can they understand life after death because without faith this cannot be comprehended.

That which is *not* seen is eternal, and the unseen can only be understood by having faith in God alone. This is what happens when one believes in what is seen only, as if this is what is being interpreted as real. Paul compels us not to do this and he says to us, "While we look not at the things which are seen, but at the things which are not seen: for the things which are seen are temporal; but the things which are not seen are eternal" (2 Cor. 4:18). Spiritual life in the Spirit is predicated upon a personal relationship with God's Spirit in faith through the

Lord Jesus Christ, and this must happen before one *expires* in the flesh. The decision to believe in God must occur before one dies in the *flesh*. *Death in the flesh* is when God's Spirit is *separated* from the body, and *eternal death* occurs when *God's Spirit is separated from the human soul* in the Spirit world. This separation from God's Spirit is what causes *spiritual death*, which is eternal.

Then spiritual death is actually *separation* from God, as natural death is the soul separating from the flesh, and when this happens, this separation from the flesh is not the end of life. This decision to choose Jesus Christ must be made before death in the flesh occurs. Even when the soul separates from God's Spirit and spiritual death occurs, when the soul is separated from God's Spirit in eternity, it still lives in eternity. It is now only apart from God, and the decision to accept Jesus Christ cannot be made at that time.

But now, this separation from God is eternal, and this separation from God is what causes *spiritual death* in the Spirit. Thus, the Spirit separated from God still lives in death though it is separated from God. There is no *death* in the spirit even though being separated from God is death. The Spirit lives on in *Sheol*/or in *hell* a part from God. In the Bible, *hell* is a place that is described where there is weeping and gnashing of teeth (Matt. 13:42), and heaven is where God is. And you are in a perpetual state of eternal bliss (John 14:2–3). According to the biblical paradigm in the creation narrative, physical death is the consequence of humanity's *decision* not to follow God's edicts and/or commands.

In this narrative, death gained access into the physical world, and, because of this, *sin* and *disobedience* caused humanity to *die* in the flesh. And death entered into the physical world. If the truth be told, there is no death in the Spirit, and though life offers us many options to choose from in the physical world, there are only two options in the spiritual realm: *heaven* or *hell*. Death in the spiritual realm is caused by one's *unbelief* in God and by not exercising faith while one was alive in the flesh. Belief in God must *precede* death in the natural (flesh) in order to live with God in the Spirit eternally and according to Paul in

Romans 6:23 when he said, "For the wages of sin is death; but the free gift of God is eternal life through Jesus Christ our Lord." The Bible further contends, "For all have sinned, and come short of the glory of God" (Romans 3:23).

Therefore, this warfare between the flesh and the Spirit is so intense as Paul contends in his position this warfare when he says in Galatians 5:17, "For the flesh lusts against the Spirit and the Spirit against the flesh" and how this one act of disobedience in the Genesis paradigm caused *sin* to enter into the physical world, and thus, sin entered into all of humanity by this one act of disobedience. Paul contends further by saying, "Because the carnal mind is enmity against God: for it is not subject to the law of God neither indeed can be"(Romans8:7). It was God who said this about humanity and her sins and how he saw her sins of wickedness as the great burden upon the earth and how her every intent of human's thoughts of her heart is only evil continually (Genesis 6:5).

Then God said this about humanity's sins when he said, "My Spirit shall not always strive with humanity, for that they also are flesh"(Gen.6:3). And this is where the *phenomenon of death* finds its origin in life and in the physical world. In this paradigm, God shows us how he distinguishes between his Spirit and that of the flesh, and how he has designated a timeline of how (*long*) or how many days (120 years) he would give for the flesh to live and dwell together with his Spirit (cf. 6:3). The point I'm making here is to establish the fact that there is a distinct difference between God's Spirit and the Spirit of the *soul*, which gives us life in the flesh; and this verse from Genesis 6:3 acknowledges this distinction here for us with pinpoint accuracy and clarity. Paul also acknowledges this distinction for us when he asserts, "For the word of God is quick, and powerful, and sharper than any two edged sword, piercing even to the dividing asunder of the soul and spirit, and of the joint and marrow, and is a discerner of the thoughts and intents of the heart" (Heb. 4:12).

However, how is it possible for some people not to believe that life after death is beyond me? Honestly, it's because of *unbelief* in their understanding that God is a Spirit and by not exercising faith in God. Unbelief is the *greatest sin*. And without faith, it is impossible to *believe* in God's word which is what the word tells us, "Without faith we cannot *please* God, neither can we come to God, because those who come to God must believe that he is a *rewarder* of those who diligently seek him, and without faith this is *not* possible" (Heb. 11:6). But when Jesus spoke about Lazarus's death in John's gospel, he referred to this death as if Lazarus had only gone to sleep, and all he needed to do was go an awake him (John 11:11).

In verse 14, Jesus shows us the association he is making with his disciples between sleep and death when he says to them that Lazarus is *dead*. Later in this same chapter, Jesus interacts with Martha and Mary who were Lazarus's sisters. He said to Martha after she said to Jesus, "If thou had been here, my brother would have not died." Jesus then said to Martha, "Thy brother shall rise again." Hence, the belief of *life after death* is presumed here in the mind of Martha. Jesus answered her though she did not understand what Jesus meant when he said to her that her brother would live again—when Jesus posed his hypothetical statement to Martha that she would see her brother again!

Although, Jesus already *know* what only he could do when he answers his own hypothetical statement to Martha by saying to her, "I am the resurrection, and the life: he that believes in me, though he was dead, yet shall he live: And whosoever lives and believes in me shall never die. Believe thout his" (cf. vss. 21, 25–26). The Bible tells us that Jesus's own resurrection would be a type of the first fruits of them that *slept*, and he, as the Christ, know that he would be raised from the dead when his time came for him to die, because he is the first fruits of those who were asleep and/or as dead and that he would rise again. In 1 Corinthians 15:20, Paul puts it this way when he said, "But now is Christ risen from the dead, and becomes the first of them that slept." Jesus is absolutely clear that death in the flesh is not the end of life and that we live on in the Spirit after the death in the flesh.

The Phenomenology of Death

Jesus makes his association of death as to when one goes to sleep and that all he had to do was go and wake Lazarus up. His disciples did not understand Jesus's association of sleep with death, as those who don't believe and are without faith cannot believe in *life after death*; and so, as Jesus said to his disciples when they said to him, "Lord, if he is asleep he will wake upon his own." But Jesus had to be *explicitly* clear with them when he said to his disciples, "Lazarus is dead!" Another example in Matthew's gospel was when Jesus restores life to a little girl and he tells all in the home of the high priest that the little girl is not *dead* but that she's only *asleep*; and all who were present laughed at him because like his disciples, the people did not understand Jesus's association of death as being nothing more than when one goes to sleep (Matt. 9:24).

What Is Sleep?

Sleep is divided into two broad types: *nonrapid eye movement* and *rapid eye movement (REM)*. Non-REM sleep occurs first and after a transitional period called *slow-wave sleep* or *deep sleep*. During this phase, the body temperature and the heart rate fall, and the brain uses less energy. REM sleep is usually when one first falls asleep, or it's the time right before one wakes up from sleeping. It is referred to as the dreaming state of sleeping. A sleep rhythm influenced by one's environment (such as lightness or darkness) as well as by one's genetic makeup determines one's sleep patterns by releasing hormones when it's time to go to sleep.

Abnormalities in the heart (circadian rhythm) can lead to a sleep disorder known as insomnia. Scientists have discovered that sleep is a time when the body and brain "shuts down," but in fact, just the opposite occurs because the brain and the body are working even harder than they do during the day, undergoing processes to restore cells, processing information, and improving one's health. This is why when persons are in need of critical medical attention in ICUs in hospitals, doctors place these patients in induced comas, a deeper level of sleep so that the body can handle the trauma it has endured and heal itself in the process.

The Purpose of Sleep

During the phenomenon of sleep, scientists have not yet pinpointed a succinct reason for why animals need to sleep every night. However, research-based studies on sleeping and its monitoring have shown that the brains of sleeping humans have given us some ideas among the many functions sleep offers. Here are three of the primary functions sleep offers:

1. Sleep offers the body a chance to recover from wear and tear of daily life. Sleep is restorative. This doesn't just mean that the body rests during sleep; rather, the cells busily regenerate themselves, and the body's temperature, heart rate, and breathing drop in order to conserve energy.
2. Sleep facilitates learning and memory. Not only do you need rest to sustain the attention and concentration necessary to learn new tasks, scientists have found that sleep is a time for the brain to consolidate memories, which makes learning new things easier. The people, who get more sleep after learning new skills, generally perform better in contrast to those who don't and who stay awake for longer periods of time without rest.
3. Sleep plays a vital role in the immune function and helps your body produce special protein called *cytokines*, which helps your immune system fight off infections. More of these proteins are produced during sleep and when you are sick, which is one of the reasons why you may feel so tired when one has the flu. Rest gives the body the time it needs to produce these infections fighting proteins and helps restore itself to wellness, according the United States Department of Health and Human Services.

In addition, sleep provides our muscles and other organs a chance to rest, though the brain is not at rest even if you are. All of your brain activity is active while you are sleeping and neurons are still firing, but they are just firing in a different way. Just because someone spends more time awake this doesn't mean that they will get more done; sleep deprivation is very costly in the United States and in the world at large. It cost billions of dollars each year in health care. There are many benefits of sleep that we just don't fully understand yet. However, sleep can only be studied in humans who are willing to participate and remain awake for long periods; which mean, sleep studies are relatively limited.

It is clear from these limited studies that there are some real health consequences for not sleeping. Scientists are pretty sure that sleep in and off itself is vital in part because it is widely believed that it is something all animals do. Sleep plays a vital function in our and other species' survival—even if we don't know for sure what those functions are at this stage. We do know, however, sleep is essential to living that even the most basic life form has to do it. So my question is why is Jesus making this association about death as if it is just like when someone goes to sleep?

CHAPTER TWO

What Is Death?

What is death? Death is an action or a fact of dying. It is the end of a person's or organism's life; it is the state of being dead. Death is the *permanent end* of the vital processes of cell life and/or tissues. Death does not discriminate, and regardless of one's race, religion, geography, or time period in history, every human or living organism *dies*. Perhaps, this is the most pondered fact about *life*, and what unites us all in life and death, it's this notion: *unification of death* which impacts us all in life. Regardless of one's beliefs, the fact remains, death is not the end of one's life, at least not in the spiritual realm. However, *death*, *dying*, and the *afterlife* are all a deep mystery, shrouded in a deep opaqueness of darkness.

Most often, this darkness is surrounded by our own *fears* or by our own lack of understandings or the *unknowns* of death. What we don't know or understand is it creates or causes in us a great apprehensions and/or concerns within us. When most people think of death, this usually conjures up ideas of our fears in our own hearts and minds. And this idea of fear is what makes death so apprehensive for most of us. It is because of our inability to control it, prevent it, or even overcome it. No matter how strong someone is or the converse, we are defenseless against death when it comes. This defenselessness against death is what makes death so mysterious, and this is the basis of our fears. And it becomes the one thing or the one idea which creates most of our fears in us because we just can't understand death when it occurs.

This is why the Bible is the *authoritative source for truth* for me, because it records God's interactions and communication with humanity. On the human's part, faith is needed when God communicates with us through his written word. And according to 2 Timothy 3:16–17, Paul tells us, "All scripture is given by inspiration of God, and is profitable for doctrine, for reproof, for correction, for instruction in righteousness: that the man of God may be perfect, thoroughly furnished unto all good works."

The Bible is the authoritative counsel of God, and it identifies God as the author of his word, the Bible. I believe there is only one God *(monotheism)* and how we get to know this God is through his *word* and *faith* according to the Bible. This is why faith is so crucial in our understanding of who God is and as the authoritative author of the Bible and how the Bible acknowledges who God is for us, as he is the one who communicates with us through his word; and this is why we should always look to the Bible for answers about both life and death.

The Mystery of Death

When one considers the word mystery and then connects it with the word death, here are some foundational questions which do emerge in one's thoughts because of this mystery associated with death: Like what are the mysteries of God's will? Why must things die, and what is the purpose of God's will in Christ? Is there really life after death? This third question is the question I am addressing in this book—is there really life after death? Indeed, death is a mystery, and so is God. Throughout history and time, humans have attempted to *wrestle* with this notion of death as we know it, and it is a subject that touches every face to four lives. And it unites all humanity under the umbrella of *inevitable mortality*. Everything that lives is impacted by death. I guess then the all-encompassing question is, Why does death exist?

In my opening explanation on the phenomenon of death, I conjecture my biblical interpretation (exegesis) and understanding of why I believe death exists. It is never God's intention when he created humanity that we should die. God never intends for us to die. We are created in his image, and we are created to live eternally with God. This is why most interpret death as being so unfair because of this inherent mechanism (how we were wired when we were created), or it's this quality (or this concept of immortality)in us to live eternally with God when he created us and while we are made in his image for the purpose of worshipping God. The subject of death is inherently connected with our *sins* and *our disobedience* to the will of God and our lack of not having faith to trust and believe God at his word which is the root cause of our not believing in life after death. I believe that without faith, it is impossible to understand death or for that matter God or how we can't even please him without it, as the Bible purports.

The Authoritative Source of Truth

The subject of authoritative *truth* is vital to our understanding of death, because without a reliable source for ultimate truth, the truth itself cannot be obtained. In Psalm 8:1–5 the psalmist declares:

> *O Lord our Lord, how excellent is thy name in all the Earth! Who has set thy glory above the heavens? Out of the mouth of babes and suckling's hast thou ordained strength because of thine enemies, that thou mightiest still the enemy and the avenger. When I consider thy heavens, thy work of thy fingers, the moon and the stars, which thou hast ordained; what is man, that thou art mindful of him? And the son of man, that thou visit him? For thou hast made him a little lowers than the angels, and has crowned him with glory and honor.*

The subject of death and faith is also inherently linked. If life after death is linked to our faith, and if there is something that does awaits us after we die, a supernatural being like God must be involved. It stands to reason why *faith* is so crucial in our understanding of life after death, because we need information to know and understand death and where then can we obtain this information from? This is why an authoritative source for the *truth* is required and is needed to help us to obtain this information about death and life after death. And why I choose faith over *religions* because faith is the common motif in all religions, and this is where Jesus's question about faith is so poignant and pertinent here.

The Phenomenology of Death

When he asked the question, "Will there be faith on the earth when he the Son of Man returns?" Though there are many religions in the world today, and not all religions teach or say the same thing. Most religions will provide you with some information on how to survive in this world, but that is the extinct of most religions, however, faith when it is understood as the *life force of God*—faith as the *nature* of God and how faith is still active even when one dies in the flesh. Many theologians and scholars alike believe that the rhetorical question Jesus raised here in Luke's gospel was about him avenging justice on the earth.

Luke says, "I tell you, he will avenge them speedily" (Luke 18:8). But the real question surmised by Jesus in Luke's gospel is, Will Jesus find faith on the earth when he returns, and do you trust him to avenge all wrongs in life? This is why I believe Jesus made this association of sleep with death at Lazarus's grave and when he raise up both Lazarus and the high priest's daughter because he was not only seeing his own resurrection in particular but all resurrections in general and how faith is needed both in the physical life on earth and in the spiritual world in death. So for Jesus, death was nothing more than when one goes to sleep, as it was when he said this about Lazarus to his disciples and to the people in the high priest's home whose daughter had died at his home that they both had only gone to sleep according to Jesus.

This is why the Bible is the authoritative source for life and death for me as the word of God. God's word is authoritative, but not only that, it is eternal. And it is the *truth*. Jesus says, nevertheless, in Luke's gospel chapter 18:8, "When the Son of man comes, shall he find faith on the earth?" In order to find a reliable authoritative source for the truth, that source which claims, itself, to be the truth must come from the truth itself—which is *God!* After all, if God holds all the *answers* to life and death, then any real answers must come from him and him alone. Therefore, faith *narrows* the situations of all religions, and ultimately all spiritual insights must come from God and can only be gleaned from him in *both* life and in death.

I believe this is why Jesus said in Matthew's gospel, "Enter you in the straight gate: for wide is the gate, and broad is the way, that leads to destruction, and many there be which go in thereat: Because straight is the gate, and narrow is the way, which leads unto life, and few there be that finds it" (Matt. 7:13–14). When family members visit another family member who is in a coma, they are there to support that member by encouraging and telling them to be strong and to keep on fighting to live. Even though that person is in a coma, it is said that they can hear those family members in the natural when they speak to them. What makes us believe that when God speaks to us in the spiritual realm and though we are dead by metaphysical standards, but only asleep by spiritual standards (Jesus's association of death in the natural as only being asleep in the spiritual realm) that when God speaks to us, why won't we hear God as when a comatose person can hear us when we speak to them.

So is it with God when he speaks to us in the Spirit even though we are dead in the flesh. Jesus says to us in John 10:27–28, "My sheep hear my voice, and I know them, and they follow me." What makes us believe that when Jesus spoke to both Lazarus and the little girl and how they both heard Jesus when he resurrected them from the dead could this have not been what Jesus meant when he referred to both Lazarus and the little girl as only being asleep, though in the natural they were both dead, but in the Spirit could they not have only been asleep? In verse 28, it says, "And I gave unto them eternal life; and they shall never perish, neither shall any pluck them out of my hand." Faith is our hope and hope as faith helps us in the future, as well as in all of our tomorrows, even in death.

CHAPTER THREE

Faith and Hope

What is faith? The Bible purports that faith, "Is the substance of things hoped for, the evidence of things not seen" (Hebrews 11:1). As I stated earlier from Wigglesworth, "Faith is the nature of God, it is God's life force, it is God's word, it is the personal inward flow of divine favor, which moves in every fiber of our being until our nature is so quickened that we live by faith, we move in faith, and we are going to be caught up to glory by faith, for faith is the Victory!" (Wigglesworth p. 741). The Bible instructs us that faith is the sub- stance of things hoped for, and this substance is God's word which is eternal from everlasting to everlasting.

So in Genesis, we are told that God *created the heavens and the earth (Gen. 1:1)*. John tells us in his gospel in the first chapter and the first three verses that, "In the beginning was the word, and the word was with God, and the word was God. The same was in the beginning with God. All things were made by him; and without him was not anything made that was made" (John 1:1–3). The physical world is created out of the divine mind of God who is Spirit (John 4:24). In Genesis, we are told that God created the heavens and the earth just by speaking them into existence, and his word become the *substance* of his faith. John's gospel tells us that God's word was in the beginning, and the word was God, that all things were made by him, and that without him was not anything made that was made.

However, in both Genesis and in the Gospel of John, they both purport and acquiesce with Wigglesworth's definition of faith, that God's *faith* is the substance of God's word found in the divine mind of God, and in both of these texts about the creation paradigm, it was

God's *life force*, God's *nature* which became the evidence of things *hoped* for in God's spoken word in creation, which was the substance of both the heavens and earth in creation. And the word of God is not only the substance of God's faith, it is a *living* power. The word of God is *alive,* and it is activated by faith when we trust God's word in our hearts.

When faith is grasped as the *divine nature* of God, it then becomes the substance of the things hoped for which then becomes the *evidence* found in our faith in God's word and in his divine nature. This faith creates for us things which are not seen, as well as the *plausibility* of life after death, as it was for God when he created the heavens and the earth by only speaking them by faith; the divine nature of God is the life force of faith, it is the power of God to call those things which be not as if they were; because God's word is alive. God's nature is acquired through faith in God's Spirit. Paul says it like this in Romans 4:17, "(as it is written: I have made thee a father of many nations) in the presence of him whom he believed, even God, who quicken the dead and called those things which are not, as though they were."

God works without materials to create the heavens and the physical world (the earth) by his divine faith and his Spirit and by those things which were not seen causing them to become as if they were. They then become the evidence of his faith which was the substance of his word and what he had hoped for in the creation of the heavens and earth. And God's faith cause the heavens and earth to become even though they were not. This is the power of faith, and why it is so critical for us to comprehend God's life force and have an understanding of faith, because this is how God's nature impacts us even while we are dead in the flesh but not in the Spirit and to comprehend how death is not the *end of life* in the Spirit. And this can only be understood by and having *faith*.

Because when God calls or speaks everything that was created came into existence by God's divine nature, and his life force demands a response which becomes his evidence of the things he had hoped for. For this is how God created the world, and when God spoke the word to produce the world, he did so without any materials except by his own faith and his word. From that which is not seen to then become the evidence of those things which he had hoped for in his creation which ultimately became the heavens and earth. The substance of his faith was the heavens and earth. And God created the heavens and the earth in the biblical paradigms of creation by faith and the power in his words.

It is an established fact that according to the creation paradigm that the Spirit of humanity is eternal and that the human Spirit never dies. And so, this is why we believe death is so unfair when it comes to our dying. And why our faith is so crucial to our understanding of who God is, and why death in the flesh is not the end of life. Our faith is critical to understanding why physical death is not the end of life and why there is still life after physical death, because God is *eternal*. God's nature *implicitly* implies that physical death is not the end of life when it comes to our dying in the flesh, since we are a Spirit contained in a physical body, and how the flesh cannot live in the spiritual domain, our faith then gives us hope even in death.

This hope in our faith works both in the present and in death. Then, this faith enables us to confront all of our challenges in life and in life after death. It is with this hope even though we are dead in the flesh that we will continue to live on in the Spirit. We need hope in death, and this is why Paul argues in Romans 12:1–2 for us to present our bodies as a living sacrifice, holy, acceptable unto God, as our acceptable (or as some others would say as our reasonable) service. This is why hope is needed in transforming our minds by the daily renewing of it and by not being conformed to this world. And this hope gives us the ability to preserve, endure to show steadfastness, and even fortitude when the days are dark and dreary.

It is because of this faith in God's word that gives us hope to face all of our troubles of both today and tomorrow, and it allows us to enter into the Lord's rest and then rest from our labors when our days have ended in the natural or on earth. This is what the Bible said about God, after God finished his works of creation, on the seventh day he ended all his works and he rested according to Genesis (Genesis1:31;2:1–2). This is the hope of every believer as Paul states here in Hebrews 4:8–11, as it should be our hope to enter into our rest as well, "For if Jesus had given them rest, and then would he not afterward have spoken of another day. There remains therefore a rest to the people of God. For he that entered into his rest, he also hath ceased from his own works, as God did from his. Let us labor therefore to enter into the rest, lest any man fall after the same example of unbelief."

Actually entering into our rest should really be the goal in the life for everyone and especially for all believers, which is to enter into our rest and not only striving for one's retirement when one reaches the age of retirement in life. Paul asserts this when he says, "For this we say unto you by the word of the Lord, that we which are alive and remain unto the coming of the Lord shall not prevent them which sleep. For the Lord himself shall descend from heaven with a shout, with the voice of the archangel, and with the trump of God: and the dead in Christ shall rise first: Then we which are alive and remain shall be caught up together with them in the clouds, to meet the Lord in the air: and so shall we ever be with the Lord. Wherefore comfort one another with these words" (1Thessalonians 4:15–18).

This is why having faith in God is so imperative and critical to our understanding about life after death and why God's word helps us to believe on those things which are not seen as being eternal as God is eternal and who has never been seen. It is our faith that enlarges our concept of the invisible God. The impossibilities of humanity then become the possibilities of God through faith, because God is omnipotent, and nothing is impossible for God.

CHAPTER FOUR

Have Faith in God

To have faith in God is the essence of what life is all about and the reason why we were put here on earth in the first place, which is to worship God in spirit and in truth. We were put here on earth to trust in God and to have faith in him. Throughout the entirety of the Bible, we are encouraged to believe God's word and to trust in him with all of our hearts. Having faith in God gives us the ability to facilitate God's word in our lives, and his word helps us *not* only to *base* our lives on what is only seen but rather on that which is *not* seen. Believing in God helps us to *bring* our carnal nature into subjection under the laws of God.

God's word then connects our faith to his word which gives us the power to overcome all the daily challenges we confront in our lives on a regular basis, and faith then helps us to overcome the power of sin which frees us from the grips of sins' captivity over our flesh as sin ultimately binds us to death while we are still alive in our flesh and then how sin separates us from God. It is sin which causes us to die in the flesh, even though we have not yet dead in our flesh. And then sin separates us from God which is *eternal death* in the spiritual realm. This separation from God is how the formation of original sin occurred in the creation paradigm as a result of humanity not obeying God's edicts and/or commandments in the beginnings in the Genesis paradigm.

Thus having faith in God helps us to overcome the powers of the enemy and as both Luke and John tells us in both the Gospel of Luke and in the book of Revelation that according to Luke 10:19, it says, "I give you power to tread on serpents and scorpions, and over the power of the enemy: and nothing shall by any means hurt you," and in Revelation 12:10, John conjects, "And I heard a loud voice saying in heaven, Now is come salvation, and strength, and the kingdom of our God, and the power of his Christ: for the accuser of our brethren is cast down, which accused them before our God day and night."

I find this to be very interesting how God refers to his word as the lamp to our feet and a light unto our path and how we are to hide his word in our hearts so as we might sin against God (Psalm 119:105, 11). Could this not have been the illumination which is needed to help us find our way in death's dark corridors? Could not this be the light which is needed to help us understand the mysteries of death's opaque darkness? And provide us with the much needed light which shrouds death in such deep and profound darkness? Here, faith teaches us that everything can happen once the heart starts believing and saying what God says, and this is the common theme and motif of faith, especially in the creation paradigm and throughout the Bible.

Could this light here associated with God's word be what is needed to help light up our pathway and be what is most significant in death along with our faith as to the reality that there is life after death? Is this the light we need to guide us through death's dark corridor? Is this what Jesus knew when he associated death with as when one goes to sleep? Therefore, believing with one's heart is indicative of one's life journey in faith as it is also about the continuation of one's life in the unknowns of the spiritual realm after we die in the flesh and our existence in the Spirit continues on in the journey of life.

As we continue to travel in life after death through the dark corridors of death, our faith is the key to help us to live beyond the natural world of the metaphysics and how God's word provides us with the much-needed light and how our faith is our hope even in life after death. Is this why life after death is a heart issue and how and why our faith provides us with this hope even in death after life in the flesh has ended and though the mind cannot take us to places where the eyes cannot see beyond the realm of the metaphysical world and into the realm of the Spirit? But how the eye of faith along with God's word can help us to live in the Spirit and in the world that is not seen?

The Phenomenology of Death

It is imperative that we understand why the heart will never follow the mind, but when an individual allows God's word to live in their hearts, the mind always speaks and controls the flesh while the heart listens to the Spirit of God and follows God's word.

And this is the root cause of the conflict between the flesh and the Spirit. Because the flesh always wants to do what it wants to do, and it is never in agreement with the Spirit of God. And this is why the Spirit will never follow what the mind wants to do, but the mind will follow the heart when it is led by God's Spirit. This is the truism found in the colloquial expressions: "Be true to one's heart and always follow your heart." And this is why faith in God's word is the illumination to our path even in death's dark corridors in our continual journey in life after death in the Spirit realm and even after death in the flesh has occurred.

And could this be why faith is so important and why this hope can only be obtained in faith through the Lord Jesus Christ? Even in death, our faith is still active and provides us with the hope to be with God, because our faith is the substance of things hoped for even in death. When our minds can't grasp the things which cannot be seen, it then becomes our evidence of those things which are not seen. So it is with our hearts as we are led by God's word and his Spirit. Because faith is required to get us to God, and God's word is the illumination to our path seven through death's dark corridors as we trust God in faith. And while we continue on in life's journey in the spiritual realm in life, even afterlife in the flesh has ended.

We Die to Live

Paul tells us that we must die in the flesh in order to live in the Spirit while we are still alive in the flesh. Without the Spirit of God, this is what makes life's challenges in the flesh the most difficult and why the challenges between the flesh and the Spirit are so intense in our lives today. What does this actually mean to die in the flesh while we are still alive in it? In Romans, the eighth chapter and the six verse, Paul says, "For to be carnally mind is death; but to be spiritually minded is life and peace." When Paul opens this eighth chapter with his explanation of what he means by "We Must Die to Live," he then says in verse one that, "There is therefore now no condemnation to them which are in Christ Jesus, who walk not after the flesh, but after the Spirit."

The process of *life after death* begins the moment we accept the Lord Jesus Christ into our hearts as our Lord and Savior; it is like the process of dying which begins at the moment we are born into this world and the battle with death commences. As I alluded earlier, this battle between the Spirit and the flesh is a lifelong one, and only through the Spirit of life in Christ Jesus is one made free from the laws of sin and death (cf. verse 2), and to experience victory in the flesh, one must walk in the Spirit of God.

No one is exempt from this battle, and no one is exempt from death. And so everyone will be required in their lifetime to make a decision as to which one they will adhere to, and then will they even follow the plan of salvation which has been laid out in Christ Jesus for them. Everyone is given the right to exercise their own *freewill*, and they can make whatever decision they prefer. But God has preferred that humanity would follow his plan based on his love for them and that he would never *coerce* anyone to choose him and go against their own freewill of not choosing him because God created us in his own image and his divine plan has placed a *divine restriction* on him not to violate humanity's free will of not choosing him for themselves. And whatever decision they would make, they would make it by their own free will.

God has determined that humanity would choose him because of his *love* for them and not by his coercion to make them choose him. But Paul tells us in verse six of this same chapter, "That to be carnally minded is death; but to be spiritually minded is life and peace." Paul here now purports that this is why it must be by the Spirit of God which rose up Jesus from the dead, and if this Spirit that dwells within us rose up Christ from the dead, he shall also raise us up from the dead by this same Spirit that dwells within him (cf. verse 11). So from these verses, Paul asserts that everyone who seeks life after death must first begin this process, while they are still alive in the flesh even though we all will die in the flesh at one point or another.

It's imperative that we become new creatures in Christ while we are still alive in the flesh so that our decision to allow Christ to reign in our hearts is done by his Spirit working in our flesh by faith while we are still alive. When we believe in our hearts and walk in the Spirit by faith; walking in the Spirit is a faith journey that continues even in death. This journey continues even after you die in the flesh.

When we do die, the death to self has already taken place which then *entitles* us to live forevermore in the Spirit with God because death in the flesh has occurred while we are *still* alive in the flesh and while we are now living by the Spirit through our faith in the Lord Jesus Christ. And so this is the *premise* of death in the flesh as not being the end of life. This faith then becomes our *hope* in life after death as we continue on in life's journey in the spiritual realm and even afterlife on earth has ended. And it is then, by this Spirit in the life of Christ which makes us free from the fears of death's dark mysterious apprehensions which comes from our unknown thoughts and feelings about death's dark mysteries.

First, faith becomes for us the substance of things hoped as new creatures in Christ even in death, and secondly there is now no condemnation to those who die in Christ Jesus. The guilt and shame associated with our sins and disobedience are now forgiven for those who die in Christ Jesus. The *no* condemnation notion now *transforms* our minds, and as Christ was submitted to the Father and was raised by the Spirit of God, so we too will be like Christ, as we are submitted to Christ Jesus. And by his Spirit dwelling within us, we too will be raised by his Spirit which was the same Spirit that raised Christ Jesus from the dead when God raised him. This is why having our minds renewed by the transforming power of the Holy Spirit helps us not to be conformed to this world as we present our bodies as a living sacrifice holy and acceptable unto God (Romans 12:1–2).

This transformation now helps us to not only to believe on the things which were seen in the metaphysical world but our faith helps us to see those things which are not seen but are eternal in the spiritual realm. This all happens when we make the decision to die in the flesh while we are still alive in the flesh. According to Galatians 2:20, Paul put it like this when he talks about dying in the flesh, while we are still alive when he says, "I am crucified with Christ nevertheless I live; yet not I, but Christ lives in me: and the life which I now live in the flesh I live by faith of the Son of God, who loved me, and gave himself for me." In order for us to live in life and in the life after death, we must have a personal relationship with the power of the Holy Spirit through Christ Jesus.

The Power of the Holy Spirit

It was Jesus who taught us about the power of the Holy Spirit and who promised us that he would send us this power after he returned back to his Father after his resurrection from the dead. Jesus said in Acts, "But you shall receive power after the Holy Spirit is come upon you: and you shall be witnesses unto me both in Jerusalem, and in all Judea, and in Samaria, and unto the uttermost part of the earth" (Acts 1:8). If it is by and through the works of the Holy Spirit that one is capable of overcoming the works of the flesh, then when the body is demanding what it wants when it wants it, this is usually done with great desires and passions about demanding those things of what the body wants.

The only way we can emulate Christ and overcome the desires of the flesh is by walking in and maintaining a relationship with the power of the Holy Spirit, and this happens when we make the decision to walk by faith in the Spirit of God. This is why Jesus said in John's gospel, "And I will pray the Father, and he shall give you another Comforter that he may abide with you forever. Even the Spirit of truth; whom the world cannot receive, because it sees him not, neither knows him: but you know him; for he dwells with you, and shall be with you" (John 14:16–17).

As I refer earlier about this warfare between the Spirit and the flesh and how Paul indicates that the only way to overcome the demands of the flesh, its desires or the lusts of the flesh, is by being led by the Spirit of God, and this is the only way of not fulfilling the lusts of the flesh by walking in the Spirit. This is every human's battle. This is what Paul means when he said *walk* in the Spirit. Paul then gives us this list of the litany of things the flesh desires when it wants what it wants, when he says, "These are the lusts of the flesh: Adultery, fornication, uncleanness, lasciviousness, idolatry, witchcraft, hatred, variance, emulations, wrath, seditions, heresies, envying's, murders, drunkenness, reveling, and the such like: of the which I tell you before, as I have also told in you in time past, that they which do such things shall not inherit the kingdom of God [or experience life after death]" (Gal. 5:19–21).

In Matthew's gospel, Jesus tells us that what defiles a person is not what they eat but by the evil words which come from an evil heart that follows when the mind is allowed to lead. "For from the heart come evil thoughts, murder, adultery, fornication, theft lying and slander," according to Jesus in (Matthew 15:19). Jesus then says to Peter in this same text, "Don't you understand? Don't you see that anything you eat passes through your digestive tract, but evil words come from an evil heart and this is what defiles a person who says them" (cf. vss. 16–18).

Everyone who has a relationship with Jesus Christ is promised the power of the Holy Spirit, but you have to make the decision to accept the Lord Jesus Christ first. When one's life is submitted to Jesus Christ, the Holy Spirit will then give you the power to over- come the craving of the flesh and such internals which comes from an evil heart and how the Spirit will influence your judgments when it comes to such things of the flesh which helps us to keep such evils away from us. The Holy Spirit will give you any and all nine fruits of the Spirit, and they will help you to counter the desires of the flesh; and these fruits of the Spirit are, "love, joy, peace, patience, gentleness, goodness, faith, meekness and self-control against such there is no law. And they that are Christ's have crucified the flesh with the affections and lusts. If we live in the Spirit, let us walk in the Spirit" (Gal.5:22–25). These nine fruits of the Spirit can be acquired by all who are in Christ, and you can have as many of these fruits as you so desire, as long as you are willing to believe and continue to develop them in your life.

The Manifestation of Faith

The whole of Christianity is contingent upon the manifestation of the works of the Spirit in our lives as believers. Many make the mistake as if they are the ones doing the work, but it is the Holy Spirit which does the work within us (John6:29). Paul argues, "If Christ has not been raised from the dead, then our preaching is worthless." Without the manifestation of Jesus's resurrection, our preaching is empty, and so is our faith. Paul asserts further, "And if Christ is not risen, then is our preaching in vain, and your faith is (also) vain" (according to 1 Corinthians 15:14, emphasis added). The manifestation of God's evidence is the resurrection of Jesus, and this is the foundation of the Christian's faith. Jesus's resurrection from the dead is the *evidence* of the Christian's faith. The Bible tells us about being uninformed when it says, "I would not have you to be uninformed about those who die, that you sorrow not, even as those who grieve and as of those who are without hope." In 1 Thessalonians 4:13 accordingly to Paul who puts it like this when he purports, "But I would not have you to be ignorant, brethren, concerning them which are asleep, that you sorrow not, as others which have no hope."

The manifestation of Jesus's resurrection is crucial to the whole notion of life after death and to our having hope in death by our faith in the Lord Jesus Christ. I believe this is why Paul says, "If in this life only we have hope in Christ, we are of all men most miserable" (1 Cor. 15:19). Without hope and only having hope in this life, it is inadequate and will only be the cause for much misery in life as well as in life after death. If Christ did not rise from the dead and our faith is not active in death which gives us hope, we will then be most miserable in death according to Paul. It is God who created and made all things, and we are made and created in his image to give him glory and to live with him for all eternity.

Despite humanity falling short of God's glory in the creation paradigm, God never deviates from his plan to create all of humanity, and his plan is to always have us become a part of his family in life after death. It is imperative that all understand that all human beings are created by God and are to be included in his family as his children. But not all human beings will become a part of God's family because not all will choose to become a part of God's family. Each individual has the free will to choose, and God has left this up to each individual to either *choose* or *not choose* to be a part of his family. And I've already discussed about our free will to make our own choices and how God has restricted himself from influencing our decisions of not choosing him. It's our own decision to become a member of God's family by making the decision to be *born again* in the name of Jesus Christ before we die in the flesh.

The decision to accept Jesus Christ can only be made while we still are alive in the flesh. Once we die in the flesh, the decision to accept Jesus Christ cannot be made after we die in the flesh. God's divine limitation has restricted him, and he has allowed humanity the free will to make their own decisions and choose to believe in God's *love* for themselves, rather than being *coerced* by God to serve him. But humanity is restricted from choosing Jesus Christ after they have died in the flesh, this is why when Jesus asserted in Matthew's gospel, "But whoever denies me before men, I will also deny him before my Father which is in heaven" (Matt. 10:33).

We can only become the children of God by our free choice to choose Jesus Christ, and, quite, honestly some will choose not to believe in Jesus Christ as their Lord and Savior, which is their right to choose, though wrongly. But simply put because someone does not choose to believe and/or exercise their faith, this does not preclude life from existing after death has occurred in the flesh nor are you exempt from the consequences of not choosing to believe in the Lord Jesus Christ and God as the creator and maker of everything in life and in life after death. There is life in the Spirit after death, and physical death is not the end of life. And this is why I find it hard to believe why some would rather choose not to believe than to choose Christ and live eternally with God. And God has left this decision completely and totally up to each individual to make of their own free will or choice, and it's their own decision to make. So when Jesus tells us in Mark's gospel, "Whosoever will come after me, let him deny himself, and take up his cross, and follow me" (Mark 8:34).

Because the manifestation of the faith occurs only when one has developed a personal relationship with the Lord Jesus Christ and is walking in the Spirit of God. And every person is given the opportunity in their lifetime to make their own decision, and the word teaches us that whoever thinks that they are saving their life shall lose it; but if you lose your life now and die in the flesh, you will save it. "For what shall it profit a man, if he shall gain the whole world, and lose his own soul?" (Mark 8:36).

Therefore, the manifestation of the faith in the Spirit is crucial, and it's critical to our understanding of the belief of life after death. Death is the result of our disobedience and sins. And sin separates us from God, and though sin destroys life in the flesh and leads us to death in the flesh, death in the flesh is not the end of life. The manifestation of faith is *required* in both life in the flesh and in life of the Spirit after death has occurred in the flesh. The manifestation of faith is the life force of God's nature.

Faith is *now* and it has always been our *hope* for tomorrow, because faith is now (today) as it is our hope for tomorrow. The word of God is the *substance* of God's faith and as well as ours. And it's the authoritative truth of God's word found in the Bible. This is exactly what the Bible means when it conveys that the Spirit of humanity is eternal and will never *die,* and this must be believed before one dies in the flesh.

So the power of the Holy Spirit enables us and helps us to walk in victory over our flesh, and our faith in God's word produces the *evidence* which creates the manifestation of God's power working in our lives. Jesus's association of death as being nothing more than when one goes to sleep and as it is when we go to sleep in the natural so that our bodies can rest, heal, and regenerates itself, so is it in the Spirit after we die in the flesh so that our Spirits can rest, heals, and regenerates from its labors (works) here on earth as well.

When believers enter into the realm of the Spirit, we enter as nothing more than when one goes to sleep in the natural. God's nature is the life force which can awaken us from our sleep when we have made the decision to believe in God's word while we were still alive in the flesh. This decision must be made by having faith in God, and we must make it before we *die* in the flesh. Jesus says, "My sheep hear my voice, and I know them, and they follow me: and I give unto them eternal life; and they shall never perish, neither shall any man pluck them out of my hand. My Father, which gave them to me, is greater than all; and no man is able to pluck them out of my Father's hand. I and my Father are one" (John 10:27–30).

God's nature addresses the mysteries of death, and Jesus's resurrection is the *evidence* of life after death. And God's word addresses the *darkness of death* and provides us with the much-needed light to illuminates our path. Our faith provides us with the hope we need to believe in life after death and to live in the life after death has occurred in the flesh, because our faith is still active in God even though we are now deceased in the flesh. And this is why Paul says in 1 Thessalonians 4:15 and verse 18, "For this we say unto you by the word of Lord, that we which are alive and remain unto the coming of the Lord shall not prevent them which are asleep. Wherefore comfort one another with these words." God's word is the authoritative source for this *truth,* and it's the source of our faith and our hope.

One must have faith in God in order to know how to *die* to *live* and why we need the power of the Holy Spirit in our lives to overcome the impulses of the flesh and to help us to walk and live in the Spirit. And every believer should have the manifestation of faith as both their substance of things hoped for and as their evidence of the things not seen, and this faith is *imperative* for life after death. Faith is our hope

The Phenomenology of Death

for the things which are not seen. There *is* life after death, and Jesus's resurrection is our evidence. And *his* life is the substance of this fact.

You must be *born again,* and this second birth now includes you into the family of God. And as a child of God, this *qualifies* you for life after death, eternal life. If you have never made the decision to become a child of God and you would like to be included in God's family, it's a simple thing to do, and Paul tells us in Romans the tenth chapter and in the ninth and tenth verses, "That if thou shall confess with thy mouth the Lord Jesus Christ, and shall believe in thine heart that God has raised him from the dead, thou shall be saved. For with the heart man believes unto righteousness; and with the mouth confession is made unto salvation." I would now like to invite you to say this prayer with me by bowing your head and praying this prayer by saying:

Father, I confess with my mouth the name Jesus Christ, and I believe in my heart that God has raised him from the dead. And by faith, I receive the Lord Jesus Christ into my heart as my Lord and Savior. Trusting in him for the salvation of my soul, help me Jesus to live my life each day giving glory, honor, and praise to your holy and righteous name in Jesus Christ's name I pray. Amen.

If this is the first time you have ever prayed the prayer of salvation which you just prayed by asking God to allow Jesus Christ to come into your heart as your Lord and Savior and if you sincerely mean and believe the words you just prayed, you are now what the Bible refers to as being *"saved."* You are now a new creature (person) in Christ. Your belief in Jesus Christ as your Lord and Savior entitles you to all of the promises of God, and the power of the Holy Spirit is to help you to overcome all of the lustful desires of the flesh. Congratulations, you are now a new *Christian* in Christ, and I pray that God will help you to walk in the Spirit everyday of your life and for the remainder of your days here on earth and in your life after your life on earth has ended.

This is what the *new birth* is all about. God bless you, and I encourage you to share this good news with others because you will need support and help as you grow and become accountable to the body of Christ.

You will need others' help and support to grow in your faith and in your new walk in the Spirit with the Lord Christ Jesus. This is why the Bible teaches us we must believe with our hearts, and it is a fact, since there is no death in the Spirit. And those who die in Christ will never die but will live eternally with God. Paul then asserts here now with the voice of triumph when he says, "Oh death where is thy *sting*? Oh grave, where is thy *victory*? (You should know)the sting of death is sin; and the strength of sin is the law but thanks be to God, which gives us the victory through our Lord Jesus Christ" (1 Cor. 15:5–7, emphasis added).

Paul clearly asserts in 2 Corinthians 5:8, "We are confident, I say, and willing rather to be absent from the body, and to be present with the Lord." There is something royal about the glorified and resurrected Christ that God confirms in our hearts when we believe he is raised from the dead. The power of the risen Lord makes our hearts burn like it did for the two disciples when they walked down the road of Emmaus when Jesus came near and their eyes were kept from knowing him. When "their eyes were opened and they knew him; and he vanished out of their sight. *And they said one to another. Did not our heart burn within us, while he talked with us by the way, and while he opened to us the scriptures?*" (Luke 24:31–32).

Paul states, "When we die and we are absent from the body, we will then be present with the Lord" as Luke purports in his gospel when Lazarus was the beggar who died and was carried by angels into Abraham's bosom and only desired the crumbs which fell from the rich man's table—when they both died and the rich man ended up in hell and cried to Abraham to have mercy and allow Lazarus to only dip the tip of his finger in some water to cool his tongue from the torment of the flames of hell (Luke 16:20–26). The point being that Luke acquiesces with Paul and that at death there is an immediate response when the soul is separated from the body, and it will be present with the Lord, as it was for Lazarus in heaven and the rich ruler who ended up in hell.

Death is not the end of life… actually, it's really only the beginning

The Phenomenology of Death

of your eternity into heaven with God or your being in hell by being separated from God because of your unbelief in God. In life though there are many options in life, but in the Spirit realm, there are only two options: heaven or hell. Your decision in life determines where you will spend eternity. As death in the natural is when your Spirit separates from your body, spiritual death is when your soul separates from God's Spirit. And spiritual death is *separation* from God, which is *ultimate* separation, which is eternal, because separation from God is *"death."*

REFERENCES

Wigglesworth, Smith. *The Complete Collections of His Life's Teaching* Tulsa:AlburyPublishing, *1996.*
Zodhiates, Spiros. The Holy Bible. Chattanooga, Tenn.: AMG Publishing, 1986.

ABOUT THE AUTHOR

Dr. Morton addresses a topic that is rarely discussed, but it is something everyone will have to contend with at one time or another during their life. After spending more than thirty years in education, he also brings more than forty years of ordained ministerial experiences to this work as he speaks candidly and with candor about a very difficult subject that many would like to avoid altogether, but his succinctness and clarity will help you to confront though questions in your lifetime you would prefer to avoid, as many have done. *The Phenomenology of Death* will help you to arrest those fears about death and assist you in answering many of your most basic questions and thoughts you would like to have answered about death. Thank you, Dr. Morton, for these very poignant but yet insightful and thought provoking words in this most provocative read on the biblical interpretation that physical death is not the end of life.

www.ingramcontent.com/pod-product-compliance
Lightning Source LLC
LaVergne TN
LVHW041551060526
838200LV00037B/1244